ASP.NET Programming.

What You Need To Know

By Richard Gould

Revision 1.1

ISBN 978-1-84728-192-0

Dedication

To my ever-patient wife; Penny Joy Gould,
who taught me not to shout!

Acknowledgments

Wonderful websites such as www.lulu.com have made it possible for authors such as myself to put their knowledge into print without having to enter the dark and dangerous would of publishing.

I would encourage others to take the plunge and have a go, its fun, testing and gives an enormous sense of fulfillment once completed.

I would also like to take this opportunity to acknowledge all those who have mentored me during my career as a programmer, you know who you are!

Table of Contents

Introduction 1
  What is ASP.NET? 1
  The Programming World 3
  Why should you read this book? 3

CHAPTER 1 .... **5**

What You Need to Know **5**
  Being a Good Programmer 6
  Databases 8
    Why You Need to Know About Databases 8
    What You Need To Know About Databases 10
    Typical Databases Used by ASP.NET Programmers 12
  Different Programming Languages 14
    Starting Out 15
    Object-Orientated Programming 15
    Web Site Development 17
  Web Servers 18
  Web Technology 19
    FTP 20
    Web Hosting 21
  The Anatomy of an ASP.NET Application 22
  Chapter Summary 25

CHAPTER 2 .... **27**

Preparing Yourself to Become a Programmer **27**
  Setup a Network 30
  Install Internet Information Services (IIS) 31
  Microsoft Visual Studio 34
  Install a Database 36
  Chapter Summary 41

CHAPTER 3 .... **43**

Creating an Application **43**
  What Does the Customer Want? 43
  Designing an interface 45

Designing a database.. 46
Writing the Code.. 47
Testing.. 48
Deployment... 49
    The Customers Site 50
    Setup programs 51
    Common Deployment Problems.. 52
Chapter Summary 54

CHAPTER 4..**55**

The Programmers Environment.. **55**
    Dress Codes 56
    The Deadline.. 57
    Office Politics 58
    Budgets 58
    A Day in the Life of a Programmer 60
    Chapter Summary 62

CHAPTER 5..**63**

Documentation **63**
    Requirements Specification Document................................. 64
    Technical Specification Document 68
    Site Acceptance Test Document (SAT)................................ 71
    Chapter Summary 73

CHAPTER 6..**75**

Product Support... **75**
    Service Level Agreement (SLA)... 76
    Types of Support.. 77
        Telephone Support 78
        Remote Connection Support 78
        Onsite Support 79
        Call Logging 79
    Resolving Issues... 80
    Chapter Summary 82

CHAPTER 7..**83**

Programming Resources..**83**
    Books...83
    MSDN 84
    The Internet 85
    Your Own Code..87
    Chapter Summary..89

APPENDIX 1 .... **91**

Books you should buy or courses you should take **91**
    Books...91
    Software..92
    Applications You Should Write 92

APPENDIX 2 .... **93**

ASP.NET Programming Checklist **93**

APPENDIX 3 .... **95**

Revisions..**95**
    ASP.Net 2 95

Introduction

T here are literally hundreds of books on the market covering ASP.NET software development, but this book is different.

Have you ever wondered what it will be like when you land that programming job? What will you actually do? What skills will your potential employers need you to know? How will you survive surrounded by all those computer nerds! You might be surprised how little hands on programming you actually do!

This book contains no programming code, instead I aim to show you what you actually need to know in order to venture out into the world and become a professional ASP.NET developer. There are descriptions of technologies, hints and troubleshooting tips which all come together so that by the time you finish this book you should have a firm understanding of what it takes to write both business and Internet ASP.NET applications and the infrastructure that is required to support them.

These are all things I learned whilst going through this process myself. Yes, I went to college and learnt various programming languages, but what I didn't learn was 'what does a computer programmer actually do?' I aim to save you from wasting your time and energy learning the wrong things by telling you the exact skills potential employers are likely to be looking for and how you can go about obtaining those skills.

What is ASP.NET?

ASP.NET is Microsoft's replacement for ASP. What is ASP I hear you ask? ASP stands for Active Server Pages. Put simply, ASP allows you to create websites and intranet sites that can do lots of really clever things!

It is highly likely that you have used websites programmed with ASP.NET many times before without even realizing it. Millions of programmers use it to program online forums, ecommerce stores, web mail, bulletin boards, portals and any other type of interactive website that you can think of.

A simple password login web page written using ASP.NET.

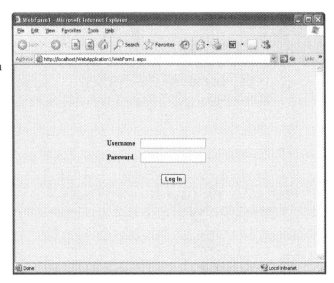

To an Internet user an ASP.NET web page looks just the same as any other web page and that is how it should be. The difference is that ASP.NET web pages allow the programmer to make use of fully featured programming languages, connect to databases and much more besides.

ASP.NET is a server side scripting technology. ASP.NET processes all programming code on the web server (in a similar way to a normal application). Once the ASP.NET code has been processed, the server returns the resultant HTML to the Internet users web browser.

There are other server side scripting technologies available but ASP.NET is probably the most widely used, partly because it is becoming the standard technology used by commercial companies to create and maintain their business intranets.

Don't worry if some of this goes slightly over your head. The important thing to remember is that ASP.NET allows programmers to create feature rich websites and intranet sites quickly and efficiently.

The Programming World

The world of programming is as large and diverse as any other profession you may care to think of. Some programmers write programs to guide astronauts to the moon, others write the code that controls your washing machine spin cycle. However, most of us end up writing applications that aid a business process and allow reporting or viewing of data and that is what this book will focus upon.

It sounds a little dull when described like that but it is the truth. Even the programmers who create websites like eBay are basically storing and manipulating business data.

In reality it can be a lot of fun, working with like-minded people in a pleasant environment. There is a great deal of job satisfaction that comes from seeing an application that you have programmed being used by a large number of people.

Why should you read this book?

Put simply, programming in the real world is different to programming in a classroom. I personally completed a number of excellent programming courses with truly exceptional tutors and this provided me with a good basis from which to launch my programming career.

But that is all it is, a basis. When you go out into the big bad world you will meet with challenges that cannot be replicated in the classroom.

This is because in a classroom you have a sterile environment where the tutor knows what is going to happen.

When you are faced with your first commercial application, you do not know what is going to happen. You will have to find out as much as you can about the clients hardware, software, staff structure, budget, deadlines and many other things besides.

All these things conspire together to make it impossible to design and build the application how it should be built with perfect adherence to all the rules of programming that you learnt in the classroom. You will have to take what you learnt and use it not as a set of rules, but as a set of guidelines.

A fundamental understanding of computer technologies and programming, specifically Visual Basic, C#, HTML and JavaScript will help any aspiring programmer whilst reading this book but even without this any reader should gain an understanding of the skills required to become an ASP programmer and how those skills are utilized by programmers in the real world.

If you are ready to try for a career as an ASP.NET programmer and want to know more about how to achieve that goal, then read on…

Chapter 1

What You Need to Know

■ ■

"Don't try to know everything, just know what you need to know and how to find out what you don't know..."

■ ■

Actually, being a hotshot programmer is not that important, surprised? These days you can obtain almost any code you require quickly and easily using either the Internet, References (i.e. MSDN), a wide range of books or simply from existing code.

Clearly you need some ability to write code, but any *"learn it fast"* book will provide you with the basic syntax skills required for a given language.

The fact that you can gain access to an infinite catalogue of sample code on the Internet makes retaining it all in your head a little bit pointless!

---

i   "**Code:** Programmers often call the syntax that makes up their program 'Code'..."

---

i   "**MSDN (Microsoft Developer Network**) is available online or with a number of Microsoft software packages. This is a great reference for programmers and includes lots of helpful code snippets..."

Being a Good Programmer

The trick to being a good ASP.NET programmer is in applying the resources at your disposal to the problem at hand.

The resources you have at hand are computer code, databases, fast servers, networks, client computers (The machines users actually sit at) and perhaps most importantly, the domain experts.

The problems you may be faced with could be anything from simply 'list our data' to 'the directors need to know our exact financial position in an instant but they are in Bermuda'…!

> **i** "**Domain expert:** A person who has expertise in the domain in which your application is being developed. A domain expert works closely with a programmer to capture the expert's knowledge in the final application…"

It will often be up to you as a programmer to find out who knows what, where they are and which format the information they hold is in. The actual programming comes later.

The reason for this is that computer applications are often conceived by managers and sold by sales men. These people are of course simply doing their jobs but they normally have little understanding of what it actually takes to create a successful application.

By the time you first hear about the plans for the new 'Super Widget Database 2006' its immanent arrival will have been widely publicized throughout the company.

A deadline will probably have been set (Usually to coincide with an event such as a trade show or product launch) and all the managers will be slapping themselves on the back for having such a great idea.

Once they recover from the backslapping they will remember that they should talk to the programmers to ensure that they understand the importance of the deadline and that it is inconceivable that the project should overrun. Failure is NOT and option!

This is where you, the programmer, come into the equation!

Ok, so it is not all plain sailing out there, but that's what can actually make the job more fun. We are getting a little ahead of ourselves here, lets take it back a few steps.

When you go for an interview with prospective employers you will almost certainly be interviewed by technical staff. One of the management types may well sit in to make themselves feel important, but it will be the technical guy who makes the decision.

Knowledge of the resources programmers have access to and an understanding of how they work will be of the utmost importance and may make the difference between landing that well paid programming job or working for a well-known burger provider!

In this chapter I will take you through technologies and skills you should focus on if you wish to land a job as an ASP.NET programmer, and those you should sideline until later in your career. I'll revisit many of these in later chapters but for now just concentrate on understanding the basic descriptions and technologies and how they apply to the life of a computer programmer.

You may well have come across many of these technologies already but ask yourself this. Have you applied that technology in the context of an ASP.NET application?

Question: "Do I need to understand the technology I am using completely?

Answer: "No, you only need to understand how to USE that technology. Let us take a builder as an analogy. The builder needs to know how to use bricks, how to lay them and stack them. He does not need to know how to make a brick! If he did ever need to know then he could just look it up on the Internet or in a book!"

Ok, lets get started with what is probably one of the most important (and boring!) technologies that any aspiring programmer should strive to understand. The database...

Databases

Databases are IMPORTANT! A large number of new programmers ignore them to begin with because they can seem complicated and uninteresting. It is far greater fun to dive straight into programming screens with flashing buttons and clever user interfaces. This is a mistake!

Why You Need to Know About Databases

Almost all modern businesses are built on data, be it a database of their customers, a database of their stock or a database of their knowledge.

Understanding how a database works and how to integrate a database into your application should be one of the first goals you set yourself as a rookie programmer. This will place you ahead of the rest of the pack and also get one of the least interesting aspects of being an ASP.NET programmer out of the way all in one go. To emphasis this point I will tell you that the first question I ask any potential programming candidate is this...

"Have you ever connected to a database through code and if so which database and with which programming language?"

This may or may not seem like an obvious question to you, but it is of first importance to me as an employer. I need to know whether the potential candidate can manipulate my business data using code.

Surprisingly few books and courses teach this. It really isn't that difficult and if you have done it once you can do it a thousand times. Just make sure you can do it!

I don't need to know if they know how the data is actually stored on the computer disk or what speed the servers hard drive is spinning at, the hardware guys can take care of that. I just need to know if they can take data that has been entered by a user of an application and save it to the database in the correct format. I need to know if they can manipulate that data if necessary and then display it to the user again.

The following scenario is typical of many real world applications.

Ex.	A user enters a search criterion into a text box and clicks the **Search** button. The programmers code then retrieves the search criteria and saves it to the database so he can report at a later date on who searched for what. The code then performs a query against the database to see if there are any records that meet the search criteria. Finally the code displays a list of results back to the user.

This may be a simplistic example, but a large part of being a programmer is writing the code that performs day-to-day operations such as this. If you can't do that then employers are likely to look elsewhere.

If you have never encountered databases before then they may seem daunting. They are actually very simple and logical. It is better when you first start to learn about databases not to get caught up too much in the complexity that can arise as you study them further.

There are two reasons for this. Firstly, as a rookie programmer it is unlikely that you will be asked to design a database. It is more likely that you will be expected to write small segments of code that link to an existing database.

Secondly, software companies often employ specialist database designers and support staff that should take care of the more technical aspects of database administration such as data backups and performance monitoring.

What You Need To Know About Databases

Concentrate on understanding the basics, you will pick up the rest as you progress up the programming ladder. As a basic guide, you should aim to know the answers to each of the following questions and preferably be able to implement your answers in the database of your choice as early in your programming career as possible.

- ❑ **What are Tables, Rows and Columns?**

- ❑ **What relates data in one table to another?**

- ❑ **Why are there different data types?**

- ❑ **What are Unique Keys?**

You can develop surprisingly complex programs that connect to a database that has been created with just these skills alone. As you progress further you will learn that most databases provide ways to protect the integrity of your data and increase the performance of your database.

They also incorporate tools that assist with important database tasks, such as the creation of backup files. Business critical applications require these additional features to protect against the losses that can be caused by database down time. Today, many businesses throughout the world are so reliant upon their databases that they simply cannot function without them.

An example may help to nail this point home.

Ex

A vehicle insurance company has a call center housing 100 telephone insurance support personnel. These employees deal with over 1000 calls a day. Each employee has a PC at their workstation so they can access the relevant data when a customer calls. If the database is not available for just one day that is 1000 paying customers who have been let down!

If each customer has a $200 spend that could be as much as a $200,000 loss to the company!

Ok, I think I have made my point. It is important to learn about databases! Companies such as the one given in the example usually employ a specialist database administrator whose role is to maintain and backup the companies' data to prevent such catastrophes.

They will make full use of the databases powerful tools and provide regular reports to the management team regarding the efficiency and integrity of the data.

However, it is you as a programmer who will have to write the program that connects to the database and you may also have a role in the initial development of the database schema as well. A firm understanding of databases from the outset of your programming career can help protect you against being the guy who wrote the insurance application detailed above!

Typical Databases Used by ASP.NET Programmers

To help you get started with this topic I have provided a list of some of the databases that are commonly used by ASP.NET programmers in Table 1.1, along with a basic overview of their positive and negative points.

Of course there are other databases in use but these are the ones you are most likely to encounter and therefore the most likely to be sought after by employers.

Table 1.1 Commonly used databases

Database	For	Against	Usage
Microsoft Access	Widely used and easily available	Limited Abilities	Small office tasks
	Easily Managed	Limited Security	Non commercial Websites
			Non Critical Business Applications
Microsoft SQL Server	Widely Available	Moderately Expensive	Small, Medium and large business applications
	Can handle large amounts of data	Harder to use than Access	
	Easily managed through Enterprise Manager		
	Widely Supported		
Oracle	Very large amounts of data	Harder to manage, although applications available	Large commercial organizations
		Requires expert Administrator	
MY SQL	Widely available	Used by relatively few businesses	Personal websites
	Free		Free commercial web sites
	Lots of free support via web		

It is important for you to understand the differences between these databases, the reasons companies choose between them and the fact that in general small companies use cheap databases and big companies use expensive databases. It is often as simple as that!

If you are just starting out with ASP.NET programming then using a Microsoft Access database is probably the best way to go. It is easy to get hold of, it doesn't require supercomputer type resources and there are lots of code examples and forums on the Internet that can prove invaluable as sources of information. There is also a chance that you have encountered this database before as it is commonly used in the home and by small companies.

Another advantage to starting with Microsoft Access is that later as you advance, moving from Access to MS SQL is fairly painless as much of the SQL syntax is the same between the two databases.

> **i**   "**SQL (Structured Query Language**), pronounced 'sequel', is a language that allows programmers to query the data held in relational database systems..."

Different Programming Languages

The more programming languages you have experience with the better as far as landing a programming role goes.

If you are specifically aiming towards a career as an ASP.NET programmer then you should focus on Visual basic and C# as these are the two languages that are most commonly used for ASP.NET application development. This book is not a guide on how to program with Visual Basic and C# and I would recommend to anybody who doesn't already have experience with either of these languages to take a course or purchase a good book that deals with that subject specifically.

Starting Out

If you are just starting out with programming I would recommend Visual Basic as it is generally considered to be easier to learn and more 'User Friendly'. Despite what old die hard programmers say, these days there is no noticeable difference in the performance of applications programmed in Visual Basic and C#. More experienced programmers may prefer C# as its syntax is closer to that of C++ and Java.

Interestingly, at the time of writing C# also tends to command higher salaries than Visual Basic.

Object-Orientated Programming

Once you have discovered the basics of programming languages it is advisable to gain a basic understanding of object-oriented design.

Modern ASP.NET programming, particularly if you use some of the modern development environments such as Microsoft's Visual Studio, is by its very nature 'Object Oriented'.

Object-oriented Design is one of the buzzwords employers like to see on your CV. In reality very few of them actually know what it means and even fewer will make use of its benefits during the development process.

That aside, having learned the basics of object-oriented design will stand you in good stead during the interview/selection process. It is really not that difficult, and is based on the concept that there is no point in reinventing the wheel.

A man in your local town has invented the wheel and started mass production. The problem is that you need a wheel with a rubber tyre.

You could build a wheel of your own and then add a tyre, but it would be much quicker to use one of his wheels and just add the rubber tyre.

In object-oriented language this is called 'Inheritance'. You have 'inherited' his wheel design and simply added a rubber tyre.

It is common sense really, and once you start programming you will find you inherit other code objects all the time. The most common example I can think of is the humble button.

Fig 1.1:

A simple button

Submit

Almost every web page and computer program has numerous buttons allowing users to save data or link to other pages. It would be crazy for each programmer to create a button from scratch when so many others have done so already.

It is far easier to 'inherit' a basic button and then change its properties slightly, the wording for example, than to create a button of your own.

As a rookie programmer it is unlikely that you will be expected to be an expert in object-oriented design. Specialist software analysts and project team leaders will often 'design' the application using object-oriented design techniques. You will then be given a small segment of the design to code.

Web Site Development

Since ASP.NET development encompasses Internet development a thorough understanding of HTML and JavaScript is desirable to potential employers.

 Question: "Can you create a web page using HTML and give it dynamic content (DHTML) using JavaScript? You will need to be comfortable with a task like this in your role as an ASP.NET programmer."

You may feel that creating web pages is beneath you. After all, you want to be a professional programmer not a website designer. The simple fact is that no matter how cunningly clever and complex your programming code is, you will still require an interface to the world so that the end users of your program can take advantage of its functionality.

Can you imagine a CD player with no play button? Likewise, it is essential that you provide users with an easy to use interface to your program and as an ASP.NET programmer you will take advantage of good old HTML to accomplish this task.

That interface may be as simple as a start button and a textbox that displays results to the user but it will be your role to create it and ensure it works. ASP.NET typically uses web pages to display content to users, as one of its primary functions is to create web-based applications. (Think shopping cart, online catalogue etc).

Make it one of your goals to be comfortable creating web pages, using style sheets and JavaScript to change how they look and behave.

Web Servers

Most ASP.NET applications run on a web server. That's right, a web server. Even if the application will never be released on the World Wide Web and is only ever used internally in a company it will still be run on a web server.

This is easily explained. Most companies have an internal network that comprises of one or more servers and any number of client machines that sit on employee's desks. By far the majority of these companies will be running Microsoft Windows Server on their servers, and Microsoft Windows with Internet Explorer on the client machines.

These are ideal ingredients for an intranet application.

 "**Intranet:** a system of connected computers which works like the Internet and which enables people within an organization to communicate with each other and share information…"

For our purposes we can think of an intranet as the same thing as the Internet.

What you need to know as an aspiring ASP.NET programmer is that the components of a Microsoft network give programmers the opportunity to do away with the old Thin Client /Thick Client conundrum and just make use of the components that Microsoft has conveniently provided us with.

In short, it is possible to create a fully functioning business application that runs on a Microsoft web server and is viewed by the users on their client PC's using the Internet Explorer web browser.

As we all know, there is hardly a computer on the planet that doesn't already have Internet Explorer or an equivalent already installed. This saves us as programmers from having to walk around the entire company installing a client program on every user PC.

If you have ever had to do this you will realize that this is a big plus point for ASP.NET application development.

---

i

"What is the difference between an Internet application and an internal business application running on an Intranet? The answer is virtually nothing. They both typically require a login screen, security, a database and a number of forms or screens that allow a user to enter and read data from. They both use the same technology to run and a programmer can use the same techniques to develop either... "

Microsoft Windows Server comes complete with an in built web server. This can be managed with a handy windows component called Internet Information Services and is a breeze to use once you get the hang of it.

You'll need to practice with Internet Information Services and understand its purpose fully if you intend to become an ASP.NET programmer.

This book only deals with Windows as a web server. There are a number of other web server products on the market but the majority of businesses use Windows servers so I would recommend learning this technology to start with as it is businesses who are most likely to provide you with an income! You can always advance to other technologies later if the need should arise.

Web Technology

A large number of ASP.NET applications run on the Internet. They can be used for any website, but are particularly relevant to database backed sites like online stores, forums and catalogues.

Even if your potential employer only creates applications that are designed to run on a business intranet they will probably still have a website to advertise their products and services. The tasks of maintaining your employers web site and managing any related data may well fall upon your shoulders so it is as well to be prepared.

FTP

One of the main differences in deploying an application on an intranet and deploying it to the Internet is the means by which you transfer the files that make up your application. Typically, when deploying your application on a business intranet you can simply copy your files across to the web server.

When deploying to the Internet (assuming your web server is remote) you will probably have to use the File Transfer Protocol.

> **i** "**FTP (File Transfer Protocol):** This is the language used for file transfer from computer to computer across the Internet..."

Fortunately you don't have to learn a language to be able to make use of FTP. There are numerous applications on the market that make copying your files across the Internet from your own PC to your web server easy. You will need a username and password to gain access to the web server but the web hosting company should provide you with this.

Fig 1.2:

A typical FTP application front-end

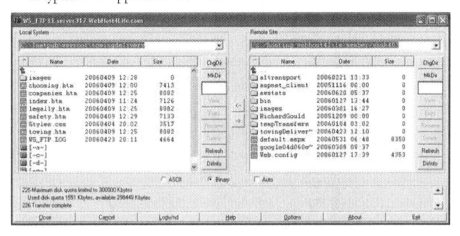

Once logged in to the remote hosts site through your FTP application, copying files is much the same as if you were copying files from one folder to another on your local hard drive.

Web Hosting

 "**Web Hosting** (also known as Web Site Hosting, Hosting, and Web hosting) is the business of housing, serving, and maintaining files for one or more Web sites.

There are literally thousands of web hosting companies out there, all vying for your business and offering deals that seem to good to be true.

You may ask why people don't host their own web site if they have a PC and an Internet connection. In fact it is possible and some people do but there advantages to using a web hosting company.

- ❑ **Bandwidth**. Web hosting companies have a very high bandwidth connection to the Internet meaning lots of people can view your site at the same time without a performance decrease.

- ❑ **Firewall**. A good web hosting company should protect your web files with a high quality firewall.

- ❑ **Security Updates**. Antivirus software and operating system updates will all be kept up to date by a web hosting company.

- ❑ **Redundancy**. Quality web hosting companies will have several connections to the Internet so if one connection is broken for any reason, your web site will still be available for web surfers to view.

In the end, very few people choose to host their own web site. Web hosting companies are extremely common and therefore reasonably cheap and financially it is probably cheaper to use a hosting company than attempt to build and maintain your own web server.

The Anatomy of an ASP.NET Application

Bringing together all the technologies described in this chapter allows us to visualize the anatomy of an ASP.NET application as seen from the programmer's eyes. Diagram 1.1 shows a simplified but typical network infrastructure upon which an ASP.NET application may run.

**Diagam 1.1 Network Infrastructure
for an ASP.NET Application**

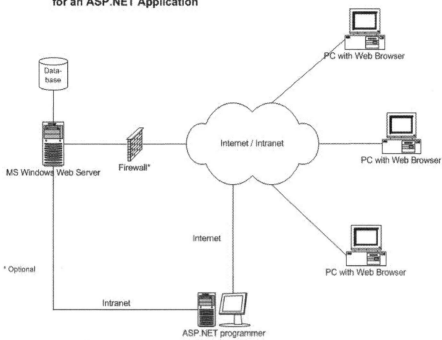

You have almost certainly seen diagrams like this before. It is a fairly standard diagram but what is important to an ASP.NET programmer is to understand what each of the components on the diagram is, what, if any, software is required on each component and where in real life do these components reside?

This is where the differences between an Internet application and an intranet application become apparent.

For example, a firewall is absolutely essential to an Internet application to protect it from malicious attack. Within an intranet it is probably unnecessary, depending upon circumstances, to install a firewall as the entire network is within a controlled environment and every user on the network is monitored.

Secondly, as a programmer you will have direct access to the server of an intranet application. You can copy files directly across the network, there is no limit on the number of files you can transfer and the risk of you losing contact with the server is quite remote.

If the application is Internet based you may have a limit to the number of files that can be copied to the server before penalties in the form of extra charges start to be incurred. Also, it is not unusual to lose contact with a remote server half way through the transfer of your files, very annoying when it occurs!

Chapter Summary

❑ ASP.NET applications can run on both the Internet and an intranet.

❑ You will need to know about databases and SQL, know the differences between the commonly used databases and how to connect to a database through code.

❑ Visual Basic and C# are the two most commonly used ASP.NET languages in industry.

❑ ASP.NET programmers run their applications on web servers, even if the server is on an internal network.

❑ ASP.NET programmers most commonly use a Microsoft Windows server with IIS installed as the web server.

Chapter 2

Preparing Yourself to Become a Programmer

■ ■

"Be prepared to spend some time and money so you can give yourself a head start over other candidates…"

■ ■

There are many reasons why colleges and schools don't teach you what you actually need to know to become a programmer.

For a start there is a wide variety of different types of programmers so schools and courses tend to focus on one topic and go into it in some depth. Also, schools and colleges are working within tight budgets so expensive, up-to-date software licenses may not be realistic for them.

Courses tend to focus on one topic, for example programming using Visual Basic. They will teach you how to write basic programs that run on your computer or how to design a computer program and these are no bad things. However, when you enter the real world programming environment you will have to be able to bring all the skills you have learnt at college and 'tie' them together into a package that is useful in a business environment.

For this reason I highly recommend that you obtain access to the facilities and resources that a professional ASP.NET programmer uses daily in order that you may learn how to achieve this BEFORE going to your first interview.

Anybody can learn a programming language but can anybody design an application to a customer's specification, write a suitable application (possibly including legacy data), deploy that application successfully and then provide long term on going support? I suspect not and being able to do that will give you an edge over other candidates.

---

i   **"Legacy Data:** Existing data that has been collated or acquired from an existing application or other source..."

Unless you are fortunate enough to have access to a facility that already has a suitable programming infrastructure in place you should think about setting up a test environment at home that you can use to teach yourself the basics of ASP.NET computer programming.

Be prepared to spend some money if necessary. Remember you are working towards your future and well-paid employment. A little money spent now will repay itself many times over once you are receiving the full benefits a professional programmer is entitled to.

At the time of writing programming provides a pay rate that is significantly higher than average. In fact a standard programmer earns more than most none technical middle management positions.

In this chapter I will focus upon the components, facilities and software that you will need in order to replicate a professional programming environment at home. Again, it is not that hard to do, but the first time you try it you are bound to encounter problems and issues. In all cases 'DO NOT PANIC'. If things go wrong think of it as great training for when things go wrong in a working environment.

I've created a quick checklist showing what you need in order to set up an ASP.NET programming environment. Each topic will be covered in greater detail in this chapter.

❑ **Set up a network.**

❑ **Install IIS on your development machine and server (free, but not available for Windows XP Home)**

❑ **Get Microsoft Visual Studio (the student version will do)**

❑ **Get a database/s (start with Access, but should use others if you can)**

❑ **Get a fast Internet connection.**

You can further increase the realism of your test setup by adding a few extra features. These are not necessary in order to write ASP.NET programs but are likely to exist on a commercial site.

❑ **Install a server**

❑ **Set up a domain**

In most circumstances an employer will have IT staff on hand to install a server and set up the network, but they may not. It is a good idea to be able to perform this task yourself.

Once you have completed these steps you will be able to start developing ASP.NET applications and then run them on the Web Server in the same way as professional ASP.NET programmers do.

Setup a Network

Most companies have an internal network, an intranet. There is a very high chance that in your career as a professional ASP.NET programmer you will have to develop applications that run on an intranet.

Even if you work for a company that only develops Internet applications for the World Wide Web, that same company will almost certainly have an intranet of its own upon which they will run ASP.NET applications during the development stage.

For this reason it is essential that you understand the basics of a Microsoft Network, that you can set and change security permissions on that network and that you understand network terminology.

i	"Often a company will have internal IT staff whose role is to manage the network. While this eases your burden as a programmer, you must still be able to converse with them at their level. They will want to know why you require changes to 'their network' and you must be able to convince them that the changes are necessary."

Ex.	You create an application that allows users to upload documents to a central location. This requires that your application can 'write' files to a given folder. You will almost certainly have to change the security permissions on that folder to allow the ASPNET worker process to perform this operation. If this is somebody else's role you must be able to explain what you require to that person and why.

Buy a good 'how to' book on setting up a Microsoft network. Create a network at home using one machine as your server and another as your client machine. This will pay for itself many times over when you go for an interview and in your new role as a professional programmer.

The machines that you use do not have to be high specification models, its possible to pick up early Pentium PCs for virtually nothing. Your development machine (The computer upon which you write your programs) will need to be fairly powerful as Microsoft Visual Studio uses a significant amount of your computers resources, but the client machines upon which you test your application can be really weak, as long as they can run Internet Explorer.

Install Internet Information Services (IIS)

To run an ASP.NET application you will require a web server. This will enable users to be able to browse to your application using their Internet Explorer web browser. Fortunately Microsoft provides a web server with Windows (Not Windows XP Home). This is often referred to as IIS by programmers and can be managed using the IIS snap-in.

---

i **"IIS (Internet Information Services):** A set of Internet based services for Windows machines including a web server. Originally supplied as part of the Option Pack for Windows NT, they were subsequently integrated with Windows 2000, Windows XP Professional and Windows Server 2003. The current (Windows 2003) version is IIS 6.0 and includes servers for FTP, SMTP, NNTP and HTTP/HTTPS..."

You can manually configure Web Sites using the Internet Information Services snap in but when you create an ASP.NET Web Application project using Microsoft Visual Studio a new Web Site (or Virtual Web depending upon the version of Windows) will be created automatically.

As long as you are running one of the versions of windows specified above you will be able to use IIS. It is possible that when Windows was installed on your machine the individual performing the installation did not opt to install IIS. This is not a problem. You can easily see if you have IIS installed by performing the following steps.

Note: These steps are relevant to Windows XP Professional and may differ slightly depending upon which version of Windows you have installed.

❑ **Click 'Start' and choose 'Control Panel'.**

❑ **Select 'Administrative Tools'.**

❑ **You should see 'Internet Information Services' in the list. (See fig 2.1)**

Fig 2.1:

IIS should appear in your Administrative Tools window

If you do not have IIS installed then you will have to install it yourself. This is quite easy, although in some circumstances you may require your Windows Installation CD.

Follow these steps to install IIS on your machine. Remember, Windows XP Home edition does not have IIS.

- ❑ **Click 'Start' and choose 'Control Panel'.**

- ❑ **Select 'Add/Remove' Programs.**

- ❑ **Choose 'Add/Remove Windows Components'.**

- ❑ **Make sure 'Internet Information Services' has a check mark next to it.**

- ❑ **Figure 2.2 shows the Add/Remove Windows Components admin screen.**

Fig 2.2:

Install IIS by selecting it in the Add/Remove Windows Components Wizard.

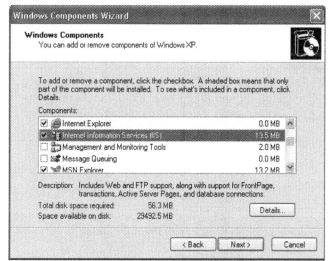

Once you have completed these steps and installed IIS you should be able to see it in your Administrative Tools window as in figure 2.1. You will now be able to host a website on your machine.

Microsoft Visual Studio

You can write ASP.NET applications using nothing more than Microsoft Notepad if you choose to do so. However, in the real world most professional programmers will use Microsoft Visual Studio.

Visual Studio is a powerful development tool, or IDE. You can use Visual Studio to develop many different types of application but in this book we'll just stick with ASP.NET.

---

i   "**IDE. Integrated Development Environment:** An application that incorporates several programs or components that facilitate the development of a program. "

Visual studio gives you the power to 'Debug' you code. This is an extremely powerful and useful feature that can save you hours of development time. If you have developed traditional applications you may well have encountered programming tools like this before and be aware of their benefits.

---

i   "**Debug:** When you debug code you can step through the code as it runs line by line and see in real time the values your objects hold. This speeds up bug fixing enormously…"

As well as saving development time by allowing programmers to debug their code, Visual Studio also has a simple drag and drop interface that allows for rapid development cycles. It is easy to drag both simple HTML objects and the more powerful web control objects straight onto the web form. You can then add the functionality to those objects by either setting their properties in the Property Builder or writing code to deal with the events that the controls fire.

Visual Studio separates the HTML element of your application from the code allowing you to concentrate on each one separately.

The HTML view, shown in figure 2.3, is similar to many web development applications with all the available controls in the toolbox on the left and the design area in the center.

Fig 2.3:

Microsoft Visual Studio Design View.

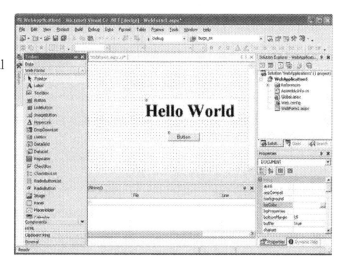

The code view displays all the VB.NET code in one place. It automatically wires the events in the code view up to the controls in the HTML view. All you have to do as a programmer is fill in the code in the event to produce the behavior you desire.

As a programmer you can switch between the design view and code view quickly and easily as often as you wish

Fig 2.4:

Microsoft Visual
Studio Code
View.

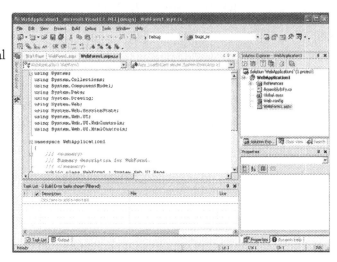

Microsoft produce a student version of Visual Studio that is specifically designed to allow aspiring programmers to sample the power of Visual Studio without the expense of a full license. See the Microsoft official web site for more details on student licensing.

I highly recommend that you obtain a version of Visual Studio and use it to create and debug an ASP.NET Web Application before you ever consider applying for a role as an ASP.NET programmer.

Install a Database

As previously stated, the ability connect to database using code and then being able to manipulate the data in the database is probably one of the most important pre-requisites to becoming an ASP.NET programmer. It sounds daunting but in fact it really is quite simple.

Take the following code example that connects to the 'Northwind' sample database that comes with Microsoft Access.

```
dim queryString as String
queryString = "SELECT LastName FROM Employees"
dim myConn as As OleDbConnection = New OleDbConnection _
        (@"Provider=Microsoft.Jet.OleDb.4.0; Data _
        Source=Server.MapPath("Northwind.mdb")

OleDbConnection.Open
dim adapter = new OleDbDataAdapter( queryString, connection );
DataSet dbData = new DataSet();
adapter.Fill( dbData, "Results" );
connection.Close();
```

You may or may not understand this code but it is actually quite simple. All it does is return a list of all the employees' surnames from the database and stores them in a dataset (which in this case is called dbData).

What is a Dataset I hear you scream? It is just a set of data that has been retrieved from the database and is held in the computers memory for easy manipulation. Terms like this will become second nature to you once you have immersed yourself further into ASP.NET

Remember, once you have used it once you will use very much the same code again each time you connect to the database. With this in mind, most programmers will put code like this into a class so they can reuse it time and again. All the class will require is that the query string is passed in as a parameter.

Before you can try out the code above you will need to install a database. The easiest database to get hold of is Microsoft Access. Many of you will already have a copy of this database program on your computer. It is nice and easy to administer and it is also used by a large number of small businesses throughout the world. You can use the Microsoft Access program to create and maintain your database, and then you can connect to that database using ASP.NET code, providing you have saved the database somewhere that is accessible to your program.

Fig 2.5:

Microsoft Access user Interface.

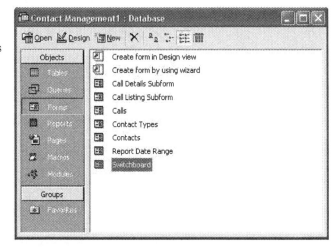

As can be seen in figure 2.5 Microsoft Access has an easy to use interface so you can add tables and data quickly and easily. It also comes with a number of 'template databases' and wizards to speed up the creation of your database even more.

For example, if you choose one of the template database designs Microsoft Access will open up a wizard that will enable you to customize the database to meet you requirements. Figure 2.6 shows a screen shot of one of these wizards.

Fig 2.6:

Microsoft Access
Database Wizard.

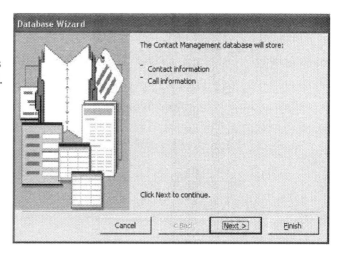

Microsoft Access also provides a good foundation to Microsoft SQL
Server, an industry standard database that is used by millions of small
and large companies throughout the world. If possible try to gain some
time working with Microsoft SQL prior to applying you your first
ASP.NET role. If you cannot do this then stick with Microsoft Access
and become as familiar with connecting to a database through code as
you can.

Concentrate on creating screens that enable users to select data from
the database, add records to the database and amend existing records,
as these are the skills employers will be looking for.

 "**Wizard:** A wizard is an interactive computer program which acts
as an interface to lead a user through a complex task, using step-by-
step dialogs..."

It is not unusual to run into a few teething errors when you first try to
connect to an Access database using code. The following list provides
a few pointers that should resolve most issues.

- ❑ Is the Access database in the correct folder?

- ❑ Has the program (ASPNET user) got security privileges to read/write to the folder in which the Access database resides?

- ❑ Is the Access Database password protected?

- ❑ Is the syntax in your SQL query correct?

If you get stuck then type the exact error message into a search engine on the Internet and you will usually find the answer that way!

Chapter Summary

❏ It is important that you gain access to a programming environment that will allow you to replicate real world problems.

❏ You will need to become familiar with an IDE (Integrated Development Environment) such as Microsoft's Visual Studio.

❏ You should practice setting up a Microsoft Access database and then connect to that database using code.

❏ Try to get Microsoft's sample projects running on your test environment.

Chapter 3

Creating an Application

■ ■

"Teach yourself the full product life cycle..."

■ ■

How does a programmer develop an application? What steps do they actually undertake to move an initial requirement through to a fully working application? This chapter is a very quick guide that aims to answer these questions.

The first thing a programmer needs to know is "what does the customer want?"

What Does the Customer Want?

It is vital as a programmer to know exactly what the customer wants and what they need to achieve as early in a project as possible. Making changes later can be very time consuming and can often introduce bugs into your code.

You will obtain this information through meetings (or other communications) with the customer and the results of those meetings will be put into writing and form the Requirements Document.

Once the customer is happy with the Requirements Document they will sign it and that document will then become the main blueprint for the creation of the application.

"**Requirements document**: A document that summaries the requirements for the application as agreed by both customer and programmer…"

The requirements specification document is extremely important. It helps prevent project creep and provides a 'plain English ' description of what the application should do.

"**Project Creep**: Also known as Scope Creep refers to the change in a project's scope after the project work has started. Typically, the scope expands by the addition of new features to an already approved feature list. As a result, the project drifts away from its original purpose, timeline, and budget. …"

Once you know what the customer wants it is important to look at the infrastructure that they want the application to run on. You need to know they have a network that can support an ASP.NET application and that you can have access to the network to install and maintain your application.

Be careful at this stage, as the people you will be dealing with are not normally technical staff. They will have a tendency to say yes to everything but make sure that you get this in writing. If at a later stage in the project you lose a lot of time because of technical issues that are beyond your control you will have the documentation in place to explain why you are going to deliver late.

Designing an interface

If an interface is required it is often left to the programmer to design it. This is not really ideal because as a programmer the tendency will be to design an interface that is easy to create and manipulate with code, this may not be what the customer requires.

A commonly used technique is to create 'mock' screens that can be shown to the customer to see if they fit their requirements. If they do not, the mock up screens can be modified accordingly. This technique has a number of advantages.

Firstly, as programmer you will create an interface that fits the customer's requirements, not just in its functionality but also in its appearance. The appearance of an application is often very important to customers. They may have a corporate identity that they want the program to maintain (colors, logos etc).

Another advantage is that the customer gets to visualize their application at a very early stage in its development. This helps to give the impression that the development of the application is progressing well. Your customers can show their bosses the mock screens and start to introduce users to what they may expect to see.

Yet another advantage is that the customer will be able to visualize the actual size of input areas on the screen. They may, for example, at this stage decide that a particular input box needs to be much larger as the users are going to need to input a large quantity of data. Being able to see the input box as it will appear on the screen will help potential changes like this to be discovered early and be incorporated in the initial database design.

Designing a database

If a database is required the information you now have in terms of the customer requirements and the user interface should allow you to create a suitable database schema.

---

i	"**Database Schema**: The structure of a database system, described in a formal language supported by the database management system (DBMS). In a relational database, the schema defines the tables, the fields in each table, and the relationships between fields and tables…"

As you start to design the database, adding tables and fields, further revisions may be needed as new issues come to light. It is far easier to make revisions now than at a later date.

It is worth noting at this point that it is considered good practice to use common naming techniques through the database schema. This allows programmers to quickly recognize a table or data type for what it is rather than having to spend time finding out. There are no hard and fast rules regarding database-naming conventions. The trick is to decide on one and then stick with it!

One common technique is to prefix the table name or column name with some characters that indicate the data type. For example:

A table called CUSTOMERS would become TBL_CUSTOMERS
A table called EMPLOYEES would become TBL_EMPLOYEES
A column called NAME would become CHR_NAME
A column called AGE would become INT_AGE

Any programmers working on the project can now tell if it is a table or a column and if it is a column they can tell the data type. They can do this without having to go into the database and look at the data.

Once a suitable database schema has been created all the ingredients are in place to start writing the code the binds it all together.

Writing the Code

Finally, we can begin to write the code. All the buttons must be 'wired up' so that the correct behavior occurs when they are clicked. All the text boxes must have limits set to stop users entering too much data or the wrong type of data.

Error checking must be put in place to catch potential problems before they cause an error in the program and if required security must be added to limit the use of the program to those with permission to do so.

Writing the code is a time consuming task so the application may be broken down into smaller components by the project manager to allow different programmers to work on different parts of the program at the same time.

If this is the case then it is important that each component of the code fits with any other components correctly. Good design will ensure that this is the case. Each component effectively becomes a black box that can be interfaced seamlessly with other components when they are connected together.

---

i "**Black Box**: In software terms a Black Box is a software component whose inner workings are invisible to other software components. Only its interface is visible to other components…"

> "**Interface**: This term is often used in software design to describe the view a software component presents to other components...."

The development teams goal at this stage will be to complete an initial version of the application within the deadline limits and that adheres to the requirements specification Document. This version will then be uploaded to the test server so testing can begin.

Testing

No application will work perfectly first time it is tested. Ideally a number of users testing the application will have no technical experience and have no previous knowledge of the system. This may sound strange but users like this are far more likely to test the system thoroughly as they will do things that the programmers didn't expect to happen.

The bugs that the testers uncover will be many and varied, but some bugs are more common than others. I have listed some common causes of bugs below.

- ❑ User has entered an unexpected character.

- ❑ A number was expected but the user entered text.

- ❑ The application has not been configured correctly on the test server.

- ❑ A component the application is dependent upon has not been installed on the test server.

- ❑ A query in the application returns no data but the code assumes that data has been returned.

During the early stages of testing a large number of bugs will be discovered but as testing continues and the programmers solve the problems the application will become more and more stable.

The application will also be tested by experienced staff to ensure that it meets the criteria set out in the Requirements Specification Document (Chapter 5).

Deployment

Once the application has been designed, written and tested it is time to release it into the wild! Depending upon the project you will either be releasing the application onto the web or installing it on a customers site.

Usually programmers will run through the deployment of the application several times on their test environment prior to attempting it on a customer's site.

They will try to replicate the customer's environment as closely as possible so that they can preempt any deployment issues.

They will also document the deployment process, particularly any complicated configuration and third party component issues. Typically a deployment document will cover the following issues.

- ❑ **Pre-requisites. (What is required prior to installing application)**

- ❑ **Copying the Web Files to the Server**

- ❑ **Configuring IIS**

- ❑ **User Rights / Passwords (Enable folder sharing etc)**

- ❑ **Database Configuration**

Programmers create this document for their own benefit and also so that an individual other than themselves can deploy the application if necessary. It is not uncommon for the deployment of an application to fall upon the shoulders of the support department, not the programming department.

If this is the case then the document will have to be official, but if it is only to be used by the programmers as a crib sheet then this is not necessary.

The Customers Site

If you are lucky the customer will already have the infrastructure in place for you to install your application. You can check this against the prerequisites in the deployment document.

You should really know this well in advance so that your time on site can be planned properly. It is no good arriving at a customer's site only to find out that they do not have an available Windows server or that the client machines are all running an ancient version of Internet Explorer.

Remember, your presence on a customers site is likely to be an inconvenience to many of the staff working there, so proper planning and forethought are important to reduce the impact of your presence.

NOTE: You may also encounter some resistance from employees at the customer site. This is not surprising as many of them will have been quite happy with the existing systems (even if they are only paper based) and will be reluctant to change and learn new technologies. It is also possible that the IT staff on the customer's site may feel that you are treading on their turf and as a result they may not be very helpful!

These are all issues that an ASP.NET developer, or any programmer for that matter, should be able to deal with in a professional and polite manor.

Setup programs

If your application includes third party components it may well be desirable to create an installation program to ease deployment. This may seem unnecessary but if you are going to install the application at a number of sites, or worse still, you have to install a client program on each users PC, an installation program may be the answer.

---

i "**Third Party Components**: Sometimes it is useful to buy a component that will perform a certain task, rather than write the code to do it yourself. If your application makes use of such a component, you must ensure that it is also deployed at the same time as your application…"

With ASP.NET it is becoming rare that a setup program is required as most components can simply be copied across to the Web Server along with the rest of the application.

Common Deployment Problems

When an application is first moved from the test environment to the live server it is common for a few 'teething' troubles to emerge. As a programmer this can place you in an extremely uncomfortable position, as it is not unusual for the customer, your manager or any number of other individuals to be looking over your shoulder as you work. If the first thing that appears when you run the application is a big red error message it is easy to panic and lose sight of the big picture. See fig 3.1.

Fig 3.1:

ASP.NET Error Message.

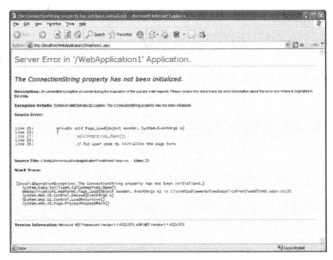

You had better get used to this message if you are going to be an ASP.NET programmer. It is often not as bad as it seems. The error message will have more detail below it. Read the error message carefully as it may often lead you straight to the root of the problem, or at least hint at the cause.

In the example shown in fig 3.1 the error clearly states that the 'ConnectionString' has not been set. An experienced ASP.NET programmer will immediately realize that this error relates to the code that connects to the database. The error message will even show the line of code or the function name where the error occurred.

Having the deployment document close to hand when you visit the customer's site and thorough preparation will help to reduce the number of errors you encounter. The following list indicates a number of common issues that may prevent a successful deployment.

❑ **User rights (folders, files):** Does your application require access rights to write or read from a directory on the server?

❑ **Web Server:** Have you created a web in IIS and set up any IP addresses or domains that are required?

❑ **Configuration:** Do you need to change any configuration settings in your Web.Config file? For example, the name of the server? The connection details for the database?

❑ **Third Party Components:** Does your application make use of any third party components? If so you will need to install this component on the server

❑ **Network Security:** Is there a firewall between the server and the browser? If so, speak to the network administrators to allow access.

❑ **Caching:** Is the server/browser picking up the latest version of your application? Restart IIS and refresh the browser (ctrl key + F5 key)

If you have planned carefully and performed a number of 'trial' deployments then the number of errors you are likely to encounter will be minimized.

Chapter Summary

❑ Computer programmers must learn the customers' requirements by talking 'Face to Face'.

❑ It is a good idea to design and demonstrate the user interface to the customer BEFORE writing too much code.

❑ When designing databases use a common naming convention for tables and columns.

❑ Non-technical staff should perform testing, as they will discover bugs that the programmers may not see.

❑ Deployment issues can be minimized by running through the deployment procedure on a test system prior to deploying on the customers site.

Chapter 4

The Programmers Environment

■ ■

"There aren't many nerds who are useful computer programmers ..."

■ ■

It's a fact. Before I became a programmer I worried that nerds would surround me. I wouldn't be able to keep up with them intellectually and I would have nothing in common with them personally.

I could not have been further from the truth. Almost all the programmers I have come into contact with are just regular guys. They like beer, they talk about girls and they enjoy the great things in life just like the rest of us. You will notice that I imply that all programmers are male. There are exceptions, but in general this is the case. I will not go into the rights and wrongs of this, it is just a fact.

Had I known what the life of a programmer entailed I wouldn't have made the mistake of assuming programmers were nerds. As a programmer you will have regular contact with clients, you may have to answer support calls, you will occasionally need to come up with 'sticky tape and glue' fixes to problems and you may even have to install the network upon which you will work, including the cabling!

These skills call for people who are well rounded, can adapt to different circumstances and relate to the customer.

Dress Codes

Everybody will be wearing jeans and t-shirt and spend half the day playing networked games, right? Wrong.

Remember, as a programmer you are likely to be working in a business environment so a smart appearance and good personal hygiene are important. This may sound obvious but you would be surprised how many people turn up to interviews with untidy hair and clothes, various piercing on their body and apparently no preparation of any kind.

I am not being an old timer when I say these things; I am speaking as a realist. The guys who run the companies you are applying for a job at are likely to be middle aged family guys and they are going to be looking for clean cut, well-spoken employees. The kind of guy they would want to marry their daughter!

There are some exceptions of course. Up and coming Internet companies are famous for their relaxed attitude to dress code and working hours, but they are also famous for their tendency to go bust, leaving you a jobless programmer!

Most of the big bucks and job security are to be found in large corporate organizations that require internal applications to aid their business processes. These companies maintain a core team of programmers to develop and support their applications and it is likely that you will find yourself in a role like this during your career as a programmer.

These companies have large budgets and often have a highly organized structure so they are good places to look for a long-term position as a programmer. Unfortunately for those of you who like to dress down, they also tend to have a smart dress code and most people working in them will wear smart business clothes to work each day.

The Deadline

One thing virtually all businesses have in common is deadlines and programming is no different. You may be the brainiest, best looking super programmer on the block but if you miss your deadline then beware!

I've seen numerous highly qualified programmers come into a department suggesting clever ways to improve the code and better ways to make the coffee but all these guys had two things in common. Firstly they always miss their deadline and secondly none of them lasted very long in the job. You have been warned!

i

"**Deadline:** The sense of deadline meaning a time limit was originally newspaper jargon and first appears in 1920. It is an Americanism. It may derive from printing jargon referring to a guide that is placed on the press to keep the type in place. This sense appears a few years earlier..."

"**Deadline:** The sense meaning a line around a prison where the prisoner's will be shot if they cross it, comes from the 1860s and prison camps during the American Civil War..."

The latter example is perhaps a little extreme. You are unlikely to be physically shot if you miss your deadline. However it is not too far from the truth. If you regularly miss your deadline questions will be asked, particularly if your colleagues are not missing theirs.

Your tutor probably taught you how to develop the perfect object oriented application, using all the correct technique. This undoubtedly is the best way to program good, easily maintained applications. Unfortunately in the real world you are going to have to throw a lot of that stuff out of the window if you want to stay inside the deadline and keep your job!

The reasons for this are difficult to explain, particularly to new programmers or programmers who have been involved with a lot of teaching. Deadlines are invariably too short and often managers want to see tangible results quickly. They make promises to other departments or customers and as a result the application gets developed in the wrong order.

Watch out for project creep if you want to meet your deadline. Managers and clients often try to slip extra functionality into the application but rarely give you extra time in which to add it.

Office Politics

Most of you reading this book will have experienced office politics. It is a fairly universal phenomenon that crosses borders, languages and cultures. But how does it affect programmers?

 "**Office politics** is a slang term for the often counterproductive human factors present between coworkers, in an office environment in the private or public sector.

It is the normal story, lots of middle managers vying for superiority over their counterparts in the other departments and unfortunately it's the underlings who pay the price. The effect on programmers is that deadlines change, projects get revised and projects that are 'Mission Critical' one day are suddenly unnecessary the next day!

Budgets

As a programmer, every project you are involved with will have a budget associated with it. If it doesn't then either you are very lucky and you work for a company with limitless resources or you work for a company that doesn't keep track of its expenditure and as a result will probably not be in business for very long!

There are exceptions of course, you may decide to write a program in your spare time that solves all the worlds' problems and take as long as you like over doing it. However, exceptions are rare and in reality companies need to keep track of and manage their finances very carefully if they are to succeed in today's business environment.

---

i   "**Budget:** A sum of money allocated for a particular purpose…"

When you start out as a programmer you are unlikely to be given a budget to manage, it is far more likely that your project manager will be responsible for the budget and its expenditure.

It's a strange thing, but middle managers want to spend their ENTIRE budget. If they don't then when next years budget is decided senior managers will say, "you don't need such a big budget this year as you didn't spend it all last year."

This can lead to decisions that from the outside appear to be crazy. Applications that have had a team of programmers working non-stop for six months can suddenly be scrapped just before they are completed. Alternatively, applications that seem to have no purpose at all are suddenly vital, provided they are completed BEFORE the end of the financial year.

It can be very demoralizing and frustrating as a programmer when these decisions are made. Months of hard toil and extra hours working to complete that 'Must Have Application' and meet your deadlines are seemingly for nothing.

Have they been wasted? No, of course not, because if you are wise you will have increased you skill set during the writing of that application. You will have learnt from the other programmers and increased you time in industry. When you enter a life as a programmer, be prepared for things like this to happen. It is life and it is what happens in business. Just think of it as great work experience.

A Day in the Life of a Programmer

Ok, so I have described the programmers' environment but I am still not sure that I have managed to convey what an actual programmer does on a daily basis. The following list breaks down a typical day in the life of a programmer.

08:50	**Arrive at the office, get coffee and chat to Colleagues.**
09:00:	**Start Work, check email and plan the days work.**
09:20	**Assuming no significant bugs or issues have arisen begin work on your current project/support issues.**
10:30	**Development Team Meeting. Once weekly/monthly the team will usually convene to discuss the current work in progress and future projects. Other issues such as development methodologies and resource planning may well crop up.**
11:30	**Back to working on current project/support issues.**
12:30	**LUNCH**

13:30	Resume work, support call has been allocated to you regarding a bug in sector G. John O'Shea has requested an account but can't log in. You investigate and discover that a single quote character causes a crash with users logging in.
15:30	You release a fix for the bug to the support department to test and release.
15:45	Resume working on current project / support issues.
17:00	Go home or for a beer with colleagues.

The above list is pretty generic. A more senior programmer may well be involved with numerous meetings during the day in which future projects are assessed, staff issues are resolved and budgeting matters are discussed.

As a result he will do less hands on programming than the rest of the team but will no doubt be under more pressure as he may be held directly accountable for any problems the project may encounter.

Chapter Summary

❏   Computer programmers need to be well-rounded individuals
    capable of solving difficult problems. They must also be
    capable of performing a customer-facing role.

❏   Most computer programmers go to work in smart business
    clothes.

❏   Deadlines are very important to computer programmers.

❏   Budgets, office politics and deadlines are all intricately linked
    and can affect a programmer's ability to meet his own
    deadlines.

Chapter 5

Documentation

● ●

"Put off documenting your code at your peril, you WILL regret it later ..."

● ●

There is no escaping the fact that if you want to be a programmer then you will have to be able to create professional looking documents using a word processor.

The purpose of these documents is to describe the application you are writing in both a technical and descriptive manor so that the application can be supported, easily used and quantified in the future.

Failure to document your code correctly can lead to problems at a later date, not just with customers but also with you personally. It is not unusual for a manager to ask you about a project you worked on in the past or request that you train a new member of staff on an existing project.

It is surprising just how quickly a project slips from your mind once you move on to new and exciting things. In such cases having complete documentation is a godsend as you can refer back to it and refresh the details in your mind.

Even more importantly, should you move on to another department or company any knowledge or detail you hold in memory will be lost completely unless the correct documentation is in place.

There are a number of documents that you will need to be familiar with as a programmer, the most common of which are listed below.

❑ **Requirements Specification Document**

❑ **Technical Specification Document**

❑ **Site Acceptance Test Document (SAT)**

❑ **User Manual**

This is not an exhaustive list, but it is highly likely that as a programmer you will come into contact with documents with either these titles or similar titles.

Your employer may already have standardized documents that they wish you to use. All the better, but read through this chapter to give yourself an idea of what will be required and ask yourself if you think you could complete the content of such a document.

Requirements Specification Document

What is a Requirements Specification Document I hear you ask? A technical and definition would be:

"A highly detailed, client-oriented specification of criteria that an application must meet, also referred to as the 'requirements document'. Often contained in a requirements repository."

In more understandable English a Requirements Specification Document is typically drawn up after the programmer/s and the client/s have had several meetings and, surprisingly, decided what is required! The client will include some detail regarding their expertise (algorithms, product knowledge, technical terms) and the programmers will tend to 'guide' them a little if they feel there would be a better solution to a problem.

Note: In some organizations the requirements document will be written entirely by the client. In other cases you may find that the programmers write this document after consultation with the client. In either case it is not unusual for the document to be revised several times before both parties are satisfied and sign the document off.

---

i   **Document Sign Off:** Although both parties (software company and client) may agree on a documents content, the document will only become legally binding when both parties have signed it...."

The result will be a Requirements Specification Document. It is actually a very important document as months after the programming has started arguments may develop over whether something should or should not have been included in the application. At this juncture the Requirements Specification Document can be pulled out of a drawer and the dust blown off. If your program does not conform to this document then you are in trouble.

It can also be your savior. Its primary purpose to a programmer is to stop project creep.

Project creep is a programmer's nightmare. Managers and customers alike are notorious for adding seemingly insignificant changes or requesting small additions to an application without thought to the deadline.

It is hard to turn down a client when they request a small change, particularly for managers who do not necessarily understand the implications of such a change.

Eventually, the change requests become numerous enough that they are significant or one of the requests turns out to require much more work than expected.

As a result programmers will (or should!) always ere on the side of caution when these 'slight amendments' are suggested. They almost always take longer to implement than originally envisaged and usually have to be 'bolted on' to the original design making the entire application less efficient and clean.

I have seen examples where management and client take adhering to the Requirements Specification Document to such extremes that the entire project grinds to a halt whilst the two sides thrash it out in endless meetings and site visits until an agreement is reached.

This makes getting this document right first time extremely important. The usual losers in such a conflict are the clients who end up paying out extra money for the changes they want, as they were not in the requirements specification document that they signed. The lesson to programmers is GET THE REQUIREMENTS DOCUMENT RIGHT! If not you WILL pay the price.

After all that it's probably a good idea to look at an outline of a requirements specification document.

List 5.1 details a basic outline for a Requirements Specification Document.

List 5.1 Requirements Specification Document Outline

Contents

History / Background / Definitions

THE PURPOSE OF THE PRODUCT

What problem / requirement it solves

Who are the client, customer, and stakeholders?

Who are the users of the Product?

PROJECT CONSTRAINTS:

Constraints

Naming Conventions and Definitions

Facts and Assumptions

FUNCTIONAL REQUIREMENTS:

The Scope of the Work / Product

Functional and Data Requirements

NON-FUNCTIONAL REQUIREMENTS:

Design and Usability

Performance

Operational Maintainability and Support

Security

Cultural, Political and Legal

PROJECT ISSUES:

Open Issues

New Problems

Tasks

Costs

The headings in the document give a fairly good indication of its content. It describes why the application is required, the problem it solves and then goes on to declare boundaries within which this can be achieved.

It really is as simple as that although in reality the document will be padded out with version and revision information and given a formal 'Look and Feel'.

Technical Specification Document

Technical specifications are typically written by programmers or technical personnel, and describe how they will implement a project. The programmers will work from the requirements specification document, and translate the requirements into their actual programming practices and methodologies.

For many typical ASP.NET programs this document will include database diagrams, software diagrams, technology (i.e. which version of Internet Explorer the program is designed for) and descriptions of the interface and its implementation.

Its content should describe the application in a way that other programmers can understand and use as a reference at a later date.

To do this programmers and system architects use standardized methods and techniques. At the time of writing a popular way of designing applications is to use Unified Modeling Language.

"**Unified Modeling Language (UML):** Short for Unified Modeling Language, a general-purpose notational language for specifying and visualizing complex software, especially large, object-oriented projects…"

UML sounds very clever and in fact can be an extremely powerful modeling technique. I personally spent many years studying the design of systems and applications using UML and can vouch for its strengths.

Unfortunately UML has become a 'buzz' word so many companies who say that they use UML or request experience with it actually use it for no more than drawing flow diagrams.

It is certainly advisable to learn a modeling language such as UML and to study the basics of object oriented design prior to setting out on a career in programming. What you will almost certainly discover once you become a programmer is that very few companies will adhere to its rules in reality.

This is a shame as ignoring the advantages of such a technology invariably leads to longer development times and less efficient code. However, the reality of the political situation in most companies means that as a programmer you will have to try to design the application as well as possible at the outset but be prepared to constantly make changes to the design and code at any stage during the development cycle.

Clearly in order to write such a document a programmer will require a thorough understanding of the entire sphere of ASP.NET programming. As a rookie programmer you may not be required to write such a document, although you may be required to give input if you are likely to be working on a particular part of the program.

You will also be expected to use the completed Technical Specification document as a template for the code you write and the interfaces you create so you will need to be able to understand the documents content and translate it into useful code.

List 5.2 details the basic outline for a Technical Specification Document

List 5.2   Technical Specification Document Outline

Contents

Introduction

SYSTEM IMPLEMENTATION

Architecture
System Flow

Risks and Dependencies

USER INTERFACE

Use Cases

Graphical User Interface Description

DATABASE DESIGN

Data Dictionary

Database Diagram

TECHNICAL ASSUMPTIONS

TESTING

Unit test plan

DOCUMENTATION

Site Acceptance Test Document (SAT)

The Site Acceptance Test Document, often referred to as the 'SAT Document', is very important to a programmer. If the application you have written passes the tests outlined in the SAT document to the clients satisfaction, then the client can sign off the project as completed.

This is a MAJOR milestone in the applications development. From this point onwards you will no longer be developing the application, you will be supporting it!

---

i   "**Milestone:** Projects are broken down into 'Milestones' by project managers. This enables them to look at the project as a series of small manageable chunks of work that each have to be completed to complete the entire project...."

Again, as a programmer you are unlikely to be solely responsible for drawing up the SAT document. The client will normally take a keen interest in this document, as they will want to ensure that the tests it contains will guarantee that the system performs to their requirements. These tests normally consist of a series of user keystrokes and actions that test the complete functionality and stability of the software system.

If the program does not pass the SAT tests successfully, and the client goes ahead and signs on the dotted line to say that the system has passed, they will be putting themselves in a very difficult position. For this reason the SAT stage of a project can be very stressful for all concerned, not least because failure to pass the SAT may result in a delay in payment from the client!

Usually the SAT document will be drawn up by a combination of the programmers and the testers and will be overseen by the managers of both departments. The managers will then meet with the client and they will go over the document line by line until both parties are happy that its contents will test that the software complies fully with the original requirements.

List 5.3 details the basic outline for a Site Acceptance Test Document

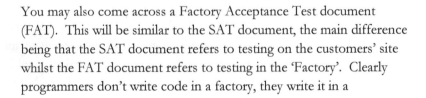

List 5.3   Site Acceptance Document Outline

Contents

Overview

USER ACCEPTANCE TEST PLAN

Strategy
User Testing

Results

ACCEPTANCE SIGN OFF

You may also come across a Factory Acceptance Test document (FAT). This will be similar to the SAT document, the main difference being that the SAT document refers to testing on the customers' site whilst the FAT document refers to testing in the 'Factory'. Clearly programmers don't write code in a factory, they write it in a comfortable office, but this is a standard term used by many industries so it is still used in the software industry.

Chapter Summary

❑ Computer programmers should be comfortable creating documents with a word processor.

❑ It is advisable to learn a modeling language, such as UML, so you can describe your application with diagrams.

❑ Documents can work for you by stopping project creep.

❑ Documents may have numerous versions and revisions as both sides approve changes.

Chapter 6

Product Support

Customer: *"I threw the old server in the trash because I didn't think we needed it any more..." (Genuine customer response)*

As an ASP.NET programmer it is highly likely that you will be expected to provide support for the applications that you have written. This may be anything from simple telephone support right through to visiting a customers site to resolve an important issue.

In reality most companies have support staff that are able to provide support to users for simple configuration faults or hardware setup issues. These support staff will only contact the programmers when there is a bug or other problem that they are unable to find a solution for.

What this actually means is that the programmers only get called in for serious issues, great if you like being stressed out, not so good if you are nursing an ulcer! But hey, that's one of the reasons programmers get paid well.

It can be fun. I personally have made a number of great friends over the years whilst traveling to different customer sites in different locations.

As you will learn, support is a role in itself. Some programmers have a natural ability when it comes to supporting their products, others will shy away from the human contact and travel that it may entail.

Service Level Agreement (SLA)

When a company purchases a software application they will often also pay for a support package. This support package will cover things like failure of the system, maintenance and upgrades.

One question that always arises is 'How quickly can you fix it?' A service level agreement is designed to answer questions like this in advance.

It will state how quickly problems should be rectified and the manor in which this is done. For example, is the software provider required to send a member of their technical personnel to the customer's site or can they simply post a CD to the customer with a 'Patch' on it?

---

i **"Patch:** Also called a Service Patch, a fix to a software bug. A patch is an actual piece of code that is inserted into (patched into) a program to resolve a bug…"

The speed at which problems are resolved is also major consideration for customers. The SLA should cover this in detail so that both the software provider and the customer can plan in advance for any problems.

Having issues like this decided at the beginning of a support contract using an SLA vastly reduces the chances of the software provider or the customer becoming dissatisfied.

In reality the management will decide what is contained in the SLA and should then budget and provide sufficient resources to support it.

As a programmer you need to know that this may have a direct impact on any project you are currently working on.

Ex. You have ten days left until your deadline. This cannot slip as the management have planned a release party and invited guests from the new customers company…..An urgent bug in an existing application is reported and allocated to you which takes two days to resolve…..You now have only eight days left in which to complete the same chunk of work you originally had ten days to complete!

The previous example describes a situation that most programmers will be all too familiar with. However all is not lost.

The key to meeting your deadlines as a programmer whilst completing any unforeseen support work is to stay ahead of your known workload at all times. This will allow a cushion for unforeseen events.

I can say that from personal experience if a manager asks me how long a project will take I always allow 25% extra to cover unforeseen events.

Types of Support

There are a number of ways in which programmers are expected to support the software applications that they write. The choice may simply come down to costs or it may be decided by security issues and politics.

Ex.	A manager of a department I once worked in would not let his programmers speak to the customer on the phone in case they said something wrong or contradicted something he had already told them. Instead we were expected to answer the question via email and only after he had vetted it! Needless to say this had a detrimental effect on the quality of support that we were able to offer!!

As an ASP.NET programmer you will doubtless come across the following types of support.

Telephone Support

Telephone support is a good idea when dealing with simple issues or if the customer has computer experience. It can become more difficult when trying to talk a customer through a problem as they have a tendency to click their mouse randomly and tell you things that aren't quite true!

You will find that your programming colleagues are strangely reluctant to answer the telephone if they know it is a support call as they have learned from hard won experience that support calls can take a lot of time and make you fall behind with your other work.

As a result programmers are rarely the people who take support calls. Many companies employ a technical person or team whose job it is to answer and log the support calls. They will solve the easier issues themselves or decide upon whom to assign the call too.

Remote Connection Support

Once a support call has been assigned to you one of the easiest ways to fix it is through a remote connection. Unfortunately there are security issues associated with this so many companies do not allow it.

If you are lucky enough to have a remote connection it will make your job much easier. You can connect to the customer's computers from your desk and look at their data and systems to see what is wrong. It is as if you were at the customer's site!

I have known times when this is a real lifesaver. Provided you have the correct account access you can even reinstall software remotely if required.

Problems are far easier to diagnose when you can see the database and error logs in real time. In reality you are unlikely to be offered a remote connection to assist the support process, but it is still worth 'Pushing' for one to see if you can get it.

Onsite Support

If you do not have the luxury of a remote connection you may find that you have to visit the customers site to resolve an issue. This can be quite a stressful experience as you may find yourself trying to fix a problem with a large number of disgruntled people looking over you shoulder!

The trick is to talk them through each step they took to reproduce the error. Ask them what was being done prior to the system failing, for example, was there maintenance work begin undertaken at the time of the failure or did they try something different with the system.

Try to be prepared before actually visiting the customer's site. By talking to the customer on the telephone in advance you may well diagnose the problem before you arrive. Then, when you do arrive you can resolve the issue quickly.

Call Logging

Most software companies will have a support call-logging system. This database is used to note the details of the original issue and to track any changes or work that has been carried out to try and resolve the issue.

In fact in a number of software companies I have worked for they have their own in-house call-logging system written by their own programmers. These systems can be used to 'train' new programming staff in the techniques and protocols used by the software company prior to letting them loose on a customer project.

A call logging system can be used to report on the types of issues that are occurring, and how frequently they occur. They can also report how long it is taking for issues to be resolved and provide evidence of your efforts to the client.

Resolving Issues

Ok, so you have arrived at work on a Monday morning only to find a series of urgent emails sent by a customer over the weekend!

They say that their job allocation system crashed on the weekend and they have teams of engineers sitting around waiting to be assigned jobs. The pressure is on!

Don't panic. Follow these steps to quickly diagnose the problem.

1. Ask for the exact error message and any error codes, these can help pinpoint the problem.

2. Ask the customer to describe the exact series of events that lead to the error. In this instance ask them the time that they received the last Job Allocation, who received it and if any problems had been noticed prior to the error occurring.

3. If you have remote access check that all programs and services related to your application are running. Check the error log on the customers system.

4. Check that the data in the database is correct. If there is data missing from the database this may well tell you exactly where the problem lies. For example you may have a table that logs emails sent by the system. If a job has been allocated but there is no corresponding email data in the database then it is possible that the email server has a problem.

5. Combine the details in the above 4 steps, confer with colleagues/documentation, and hopefully arrive at the solution!

---

i | "**Error Log:** Windows servers contain an event viewer application. If your program crashes or causes a problem it should be designed to write to the event viewer. Not all programs have access to this log. If this is the case your program should write errors to a file AND the database."

Good error logging is crucial if you do not want to waste countless hours tracking down bugs in your code.

It is so easy to rush code and cut corners with error logging but you will always pay the price later.

Design some nice reusable code that can be used throughout your program that will log errors in a concise and easily understood manor.

Chapter Summary

☐ Software Development companies will usually have a Service Level Agreement with their customers.

☐ Most support calls can be resolved by telephone / email.

☐ Programmers are not usually required to take support calls directly; they will be assigned to the support call if required.

☐ Visiting customer sites can be daunting. The trick is to try and know what the issue us before you arrive.

☐ Design your code so that it will create a Log of any errors or problems. This will save a great deal of time in the long run.

Chapter 7

Programming Resources

O ne of the biggest mistakes I made as a rookie programmer was constantly trying to reinvent the wheel. By that I mean I would spend hours trying to figure out how to do things and go through endless frustrations before finally making progress. Unsurprisingly I often gave up before finishing. I didn't realize I was missing out on some of the greatest sources of information out there.

Books

Of course, I had books, and they were useful to a point, but they never seemed to have the level of detail I required.

Books are great for getting you started and teaching you your first 'Hello World' application. At the other extreme, experienced programmers will often use advanced level books to learn about the latest technologies or as references. Where books are less helpful is in the middle ground, the 'bread and butter' programming.

If you are just getting started in ASP.NET programming, you could do a lot worse than buying one of those 'learn it fast for idiot' type books. This will give you a ground level understanding of the programming languages required and provide you with some basic sample programs to experiment with. They should also familiarize you with a lot of programming terminology and techniques.

These books often come with a CD that contains lots of useful resources such as sample projects and programming utilities.

Once you begin to write some applications of your own you will start to notice the limitations of books. You will come across problems that the author of the book did not think about or have the space to cover.

It can be quite time-consuming thumbing through the many pages in a book trying to find one specific answer amongst all the other information.

When you reach this point it is probably time to expand your sources of information.

MSDN

The next source of information available to you is the Microsoft Developer Network (MSDN). This is often supplied with Microsoft development packages and can be installed from CD.

It is a large catalogue of technical reference material, managed by Microsoft, which covers all Microsoft products and services.

In fact, it holds so much data that it is possible to be a little overwhelmed by its contents and it is important to remember to be specific with your search criteria and patient sifting through the results if you wish to benefit from its content.

Fig 7.1:

The MSDN
Website.

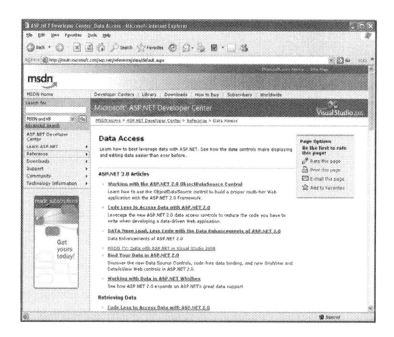

A simple search can reveal countless results, including code snippets
that you can 'cut-n-paste' straight into your own project.

One tip is to bookmark areas that you feel are useful and relevant so
you can quickly find them again if you need to.

If you do not have a copy of MSDN on disk then all is not lost. You
can access it on the Internet…

The Internet

There should be a statue raised in honor of the guys who created the
Internet. Used properly it is the most valuable and endless source of
information available to anyone in the world. It is the Internet that
made it possible for me, and thousands like, me to become
programmers.

In short, any programmer, anywhere in the world, can instantaneously (assuming a decent connection!) gain access to the knowledge of all the other millions of programmers who choose to partake. This information is free and virtually limitless, although it is considered polite to contribute your own knowledge in return.

> i "At the time of writing research shows that over 785 million people use the Internet world wide. If you assume that 1 in 100 of those is a programmer or computer professional then there are at least 7.85 million brains from which you can suck knowledge!"

The best online sources are forums and groups, some require you to sign up, others are freely available for viewing although you may have to register to contribute. At the time of writing the following sites are commonly used.

- ❏ **groups.google.com**
- ❏ **google.com**
- ❏ **code project.com**
- ❏ **gotdotnet.com**
- ❏ **aspcode.net**
- ❏ **msdn.microsoft.com**

Once you start to search for code on the Internet you will come across many more similar sites and probably begin to partake in the forums yourself.

Whenever I come across a programming, networking, installation or life problem I turn to the Internet and within ten minutes I usually have my answer. In fact, I simply can't understand why everybody doesn't do it.

For example, I recently encountered an experienced programmer in the work environment. The programmer in question had many years experience and had been around the block. He had encountered a problem and had been stuck for some time.

Eventually, with some reluctance, he asked if I could take a look. I had no idea how to solve his problem and suggested he searched 'Google Groups' to find his answer. To my amazement he had never heard of Google Groups and of course he found his answer soon afterwards.

If you are new to programming then of course I would not necessarily expect you to have heard of or used such a resource but as an experienced programmer you will find you make use of such resources time and time again.

Using the Internet in this way has the advantage of making your boss think that you are a programming guru as you seem to come up with answers to any question in just a few minutes!

Your Own Code

It is a good idea to keep all your good code snippets in one place on your development PC so you can access them easily and quickly when you require them.

This could be as simple as a folder containing alphabetically ordered files, so you can get to your code quickly and easily.

Fig 7.2:

Keep a library
of your own
code.

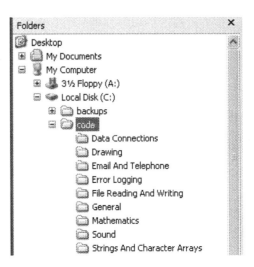

I keep a library like this and I take it with me on CD if I move job or
department. Whenever I write some new code that performs a
particularly useful function I add it to the library so that I will have it
close to hand in the future.

Of particular note, if you devise a cunning and devious plan that
involves some very clever code, a lot of trickery and handful of luck to
navigate that 'Year 3000' issue, MAKE SURE YOU DOCUMENT IT
NOW! You can be sure that in a years time when a manager asks you
to document it for a new member of staff you will not remember how
you did it or possibly even why. You have been warned!

Chapter Summary

❑ Books are great for an introduction to programming or as reference material for experienced programmers.

❑ Use the MSDN and the Internet to solve tricky programming problems quickly.

❑ Keep a library of your code in an easily accessible folder on your development computer so that you may use it again.

❑ Participate in online forums and knowledge bases.

Appendix 1

Books you should buy or courses you should take

Ok, so we have delved through what you should learn, what to expect when you become a programmer and how to survive once you get that role.

I'm now going to list a number of book types that you should aim to get your hands on and understand, the software you should own and install and the types of application you should try to write to test your newfound skills.

Much of the content of this section has been touched on in previous chapters but this summary should provide a quick and simple guide.

Books

Fools Guide to VB.NET (or similar)

Fools Guide to ASP.NET (or similar)

Fools Guide to IIS (Internet Information Services) (or similar)

Fools Guide to Microsoft Access (or similar)

Fools Guide to SQL (or similar)

Software

Microsoft Windows XP Professional (minimum, try to get a server edition as well)

Microsoft Access

Microsoft Visual Studio .NET (Latest Version)

Microsoft SQL Server (Recommended but expensive)

Applications You Should Write

E-commerce Shop

Customer Database

Support Call Logging system

Forum

The goal here is to learn the fundamentals of professional programming, not just ASP.NET but also the Server, the Database and the type of application you are likely to have to write in a real world environment.

Appendix 2

ASP.NET Programming Checklist

1. Install IIS

2. Install a Programming IDE (i.e. Visual studio)

3. Install a Database

4. Learn the ASP.NET Language basics

5. Learn SQL Syntax basics

6. Invent or select an application and write a Requirements Document for it

7. Write a Technical Specification for the application

8. Write the code to implement the application

9. Release it all to a test system and test

10. You are now an ASP.NET Programmer!

Appendix 3

Revisions

ASP.Net 2

At the time of writing Microsoft are in the process of rolling out ASP.NET 2.

There are a number of differences between this new version of dot net and the old version. These differences should not affect you heavily as a programmer, the same basic rules regarding understanding web servers and databases still apply.

The best part about this is that Microsoft has ironed out a number of issues associated with ASP.NET and they now provide a free, downloadable, Express Edition of the Visual Studio IDE. This is great news for aspiring programmers as you can now get to grips with this powerful technology without the expenditure originally required.

To get hold of this version simply navigate your web browser to http://msdn.microsoft.com/vstudio/express/ and you can download the latest version to your development PC.